Little Skill Seekers

COLORS & SHAPES

SCHOLASTIC

New York • Toronto • London • Auckland • Sydney • New Delhi
Mexico City • Hong Kong • Buenos Aires

Cover Design: Tannaz Fassihi
Cover Illustration: Michael Robertson
Interior Design: Mina Chen
Interior Illustration: Doug Jones

ISBN: 978-1-338-25555-3
First printing, June 2018.

2 3 4 5 6 7 8 9 10   40   24 23 22 21 20

Dear Parent,

Welcome to *Little Skill Seekers: Colors & Shapes*! Differentiating colors and shapes is the basis of cognitive development—this workbook will help your child develop these skills.

Help your little skill seeker build a strong foundation for learning by choosing more books in the Little Skill Seekers series. The exciting and colorful workbooks in the series are designed to set your child on the path to success. Each book targets essential skills important to your child's development.

Here are some key features of *Little Skill Seekers: Colors & Shapes* and the other workbooks in this series:

- Filled with colorful illustrations that make learning fun and playful

- Provides plenty of opportunity to practice essential skills

- Builds independence as children work through the pages on their own, at their own pace

- Comes in a perfect size that fits easily in a backpack for practice on the go

Now let's get started on this journey to help your child become a successful, lifelong learner!

—The Editors

red

Trace and write the word red.

red   red

Circle the things that are red.

Color the objects that are red in real life.

What color are strawberries? _____

_____

Strawberries are _____

Color the strawberry. Draw your own strawberry.

yellow

Trace and write the word yellow.

Circle the things that are yellow.

Color the objects that are yellow in real life.

What color is the sun?

The sun is _____

Color the sun. Draw your own sun.

blue

Trace and write the word blue.

Circle the things that are blue.

Color the objects that are blue in real life.

What color are blueberries?

_____

- -

Blueberries are _____

Color the blueberry. Draw your own blueberry.

green

Trace and write the word green.

Circle the things that are green.

Color the objects that are green in real life.

What color are peas? _____

_____

Peas are _____

Color the peas. Draw your own peas.

Color by number.

1 red   **2 yellow**   **3 blue**   **4 green**

Match each picture with a color word.
Color the pictures. Write the word.

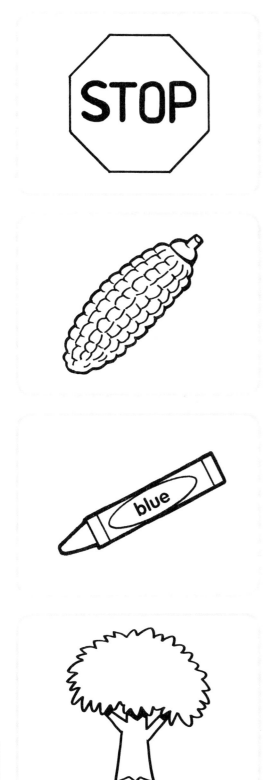

blue
_____
- - - - - - -
_____

green
_____
- - - - - - -
_____

red
_____
- - - - - - -
_____

yellow
_____
- - - - - - -
_____

orange

Trace and write the word orange.

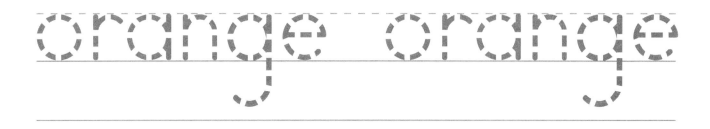

Circle the things that are orange.

Color the objects that are orange in real life.

What color are carrots? _____

_____

Carrots are _____

Color the carrot. Draw your own carrot.

purple

Trace and write the word purple.

purple purple

Circle the things that are purple.

Color the objects that are purple in real life.

What color are eggplants? _____

_____

Eggplants are ------------------

Color the eggplant. Draw your own eggplant.

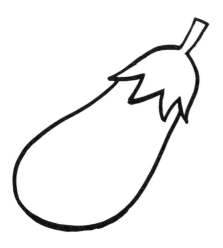

brown

Trace and write the word brown.

Circle the things that are brown.

Color the objects that are brown in real life.

What color are potatoes?

Potatoes are _____

Color the potato. Draw your own potato.

black

Trace and write the word black.

Circle the things that are black.

Color the objects that are black in real life.

What color are car tires? _____

_____

Car tires are _____

Color the tire. Draw your own tire.

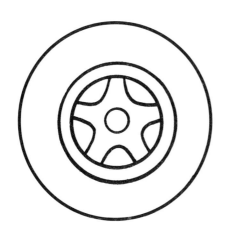

Color by number.

1 orange	2 purple	3 brown	4 black

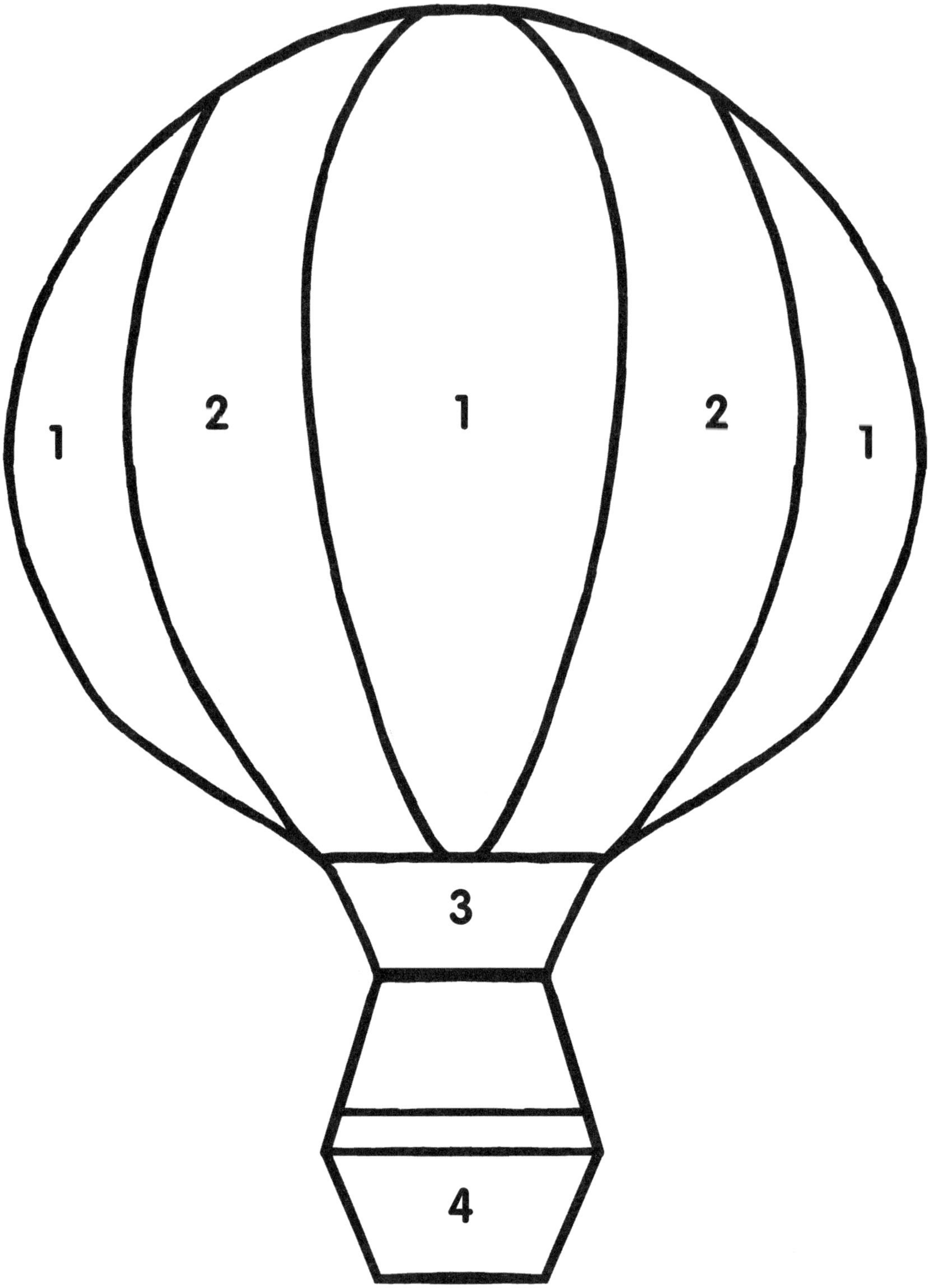

1

2

1

2

1

3

4

Match each picture with a color word.
Color the pictures. Write the word.

orange

_____

- - - - - - - - - - - -

_____

purple

_____

- - - - - - - - - - - -

_____

brown

_____

- - - - - - - - - - - -

_____

black

_____

- - - - - - - - - - - -

_____

Review all colors

Match each picture with a color.
Color the pictures.

Color each fish.
Use the colors below.

yellow

blue

black

red

purple

green

brown

orange

Trace each circle.

Trace and write.

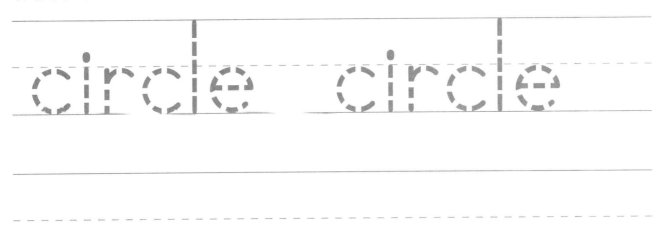

Color each circle red.

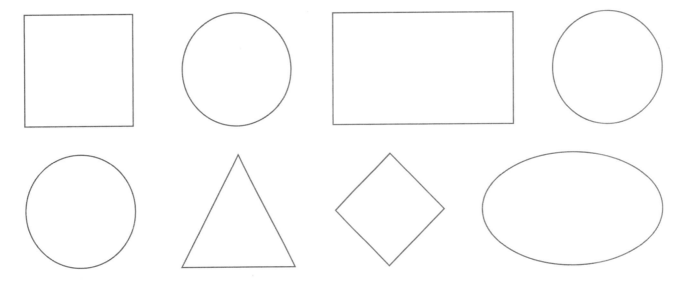

Trace the circles. Then color the picture.

Trace each square.

Trace and write.

Color each square purple.

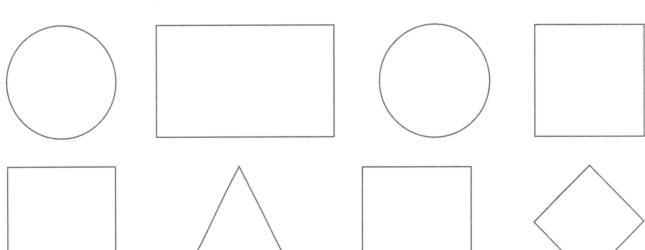

Trace the squares. Then color the picture.

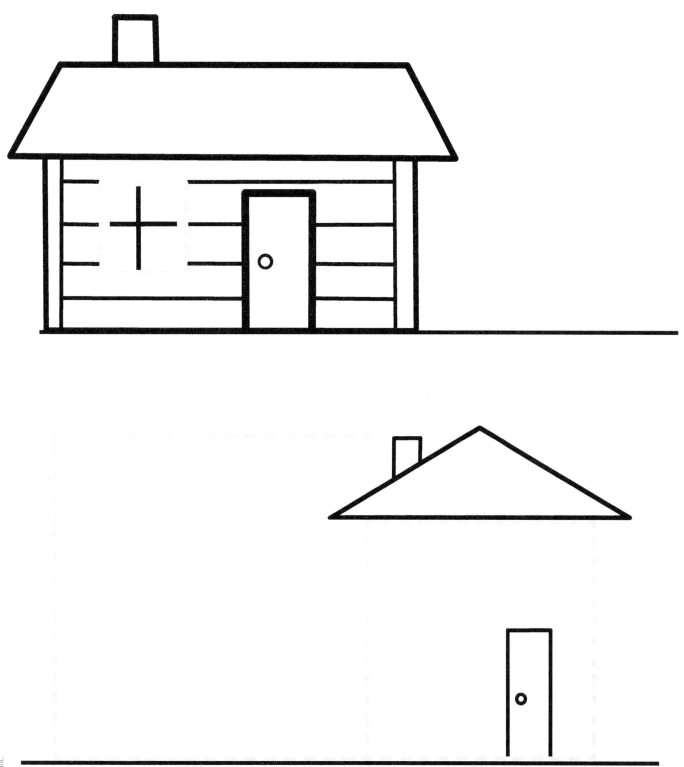

29

Trace each rectangle.

Trace and write.

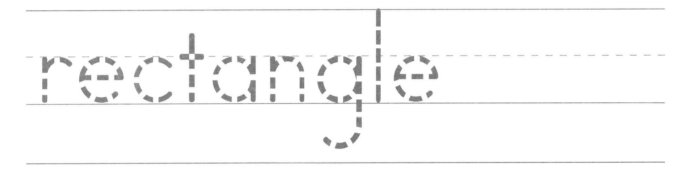

rectangle

Color each rectangle green.

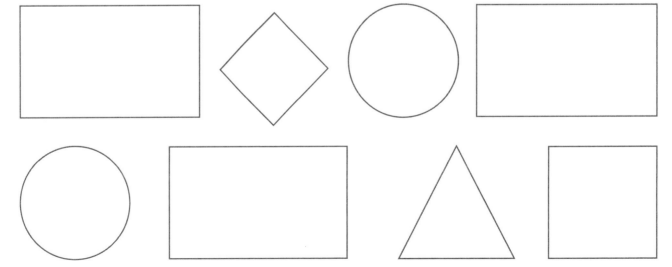

Trace the rectangles. Then color the picture.

Trace each triangle.

Trace and write.

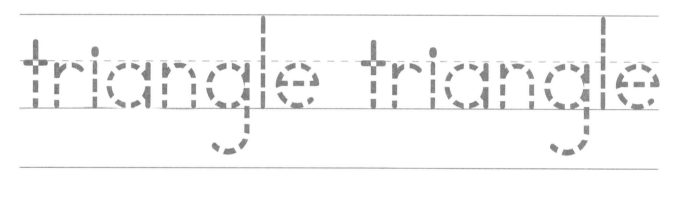

Color each triangle orange.

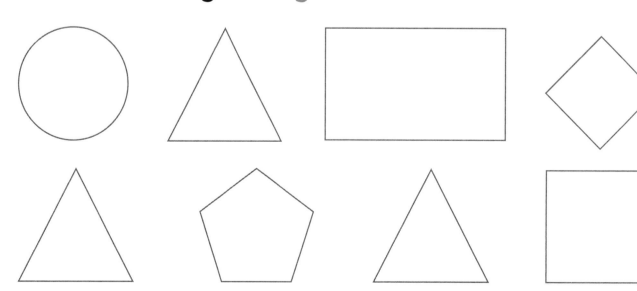

Trace the triangles. Then color the picture.

Color the picture. Use the color key.

red   purple   green   orange

Draw a line to match the shape to its name.
Write the name.

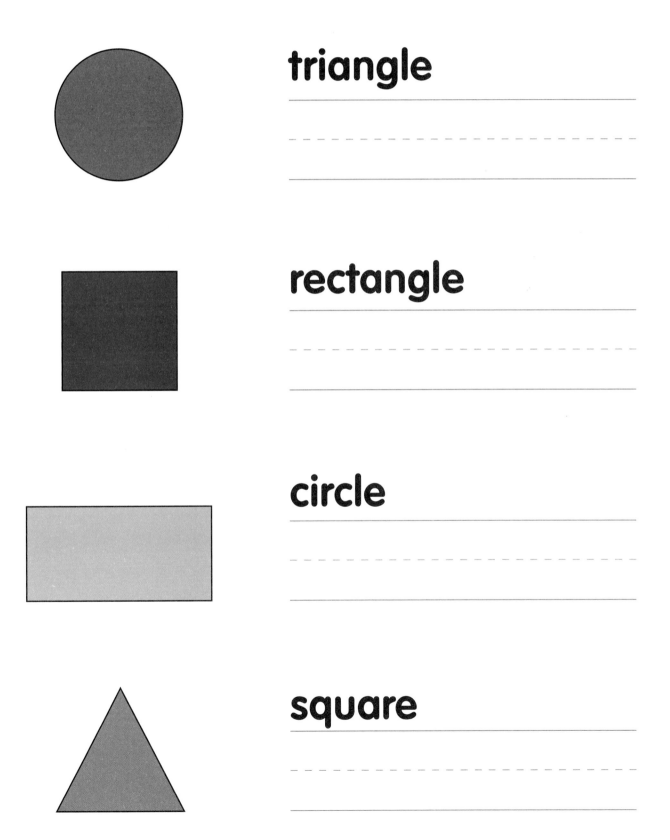

triangle

_____

- - - - - - - - - - - - - - - - -

_____

rectangle

_____

- - - - - - - - - - - - - - - - -

_____

circle

_____

- - - - - - - - - - - - - - - - -

_____

square

_____

- - - - - - - - - - - - - - - - -

_____

Trace each diamond.

Trace and write.

Color each diamond pink.

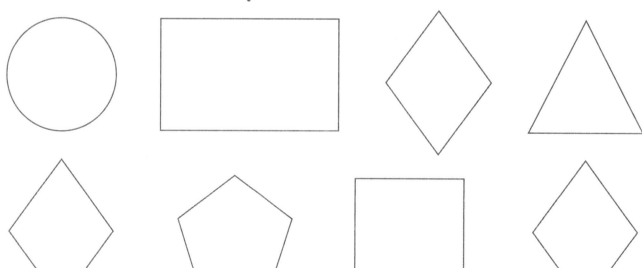

Trace the diamonds. Then color the picture.

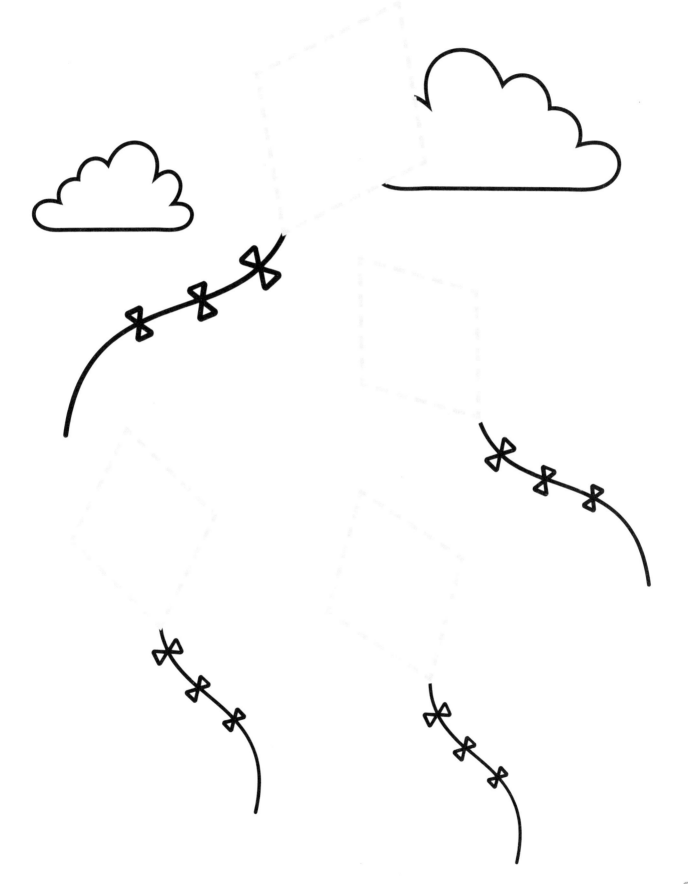

Trace each oval.

Trace and write.

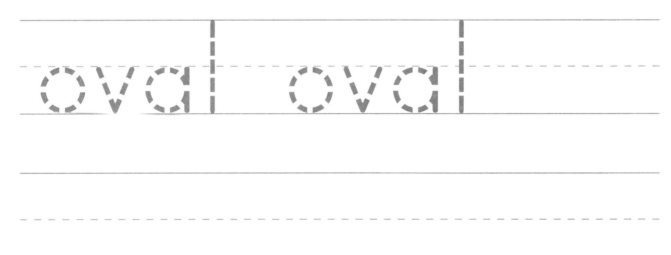

oval oval

Color each oval blue.

Trace the ovals. Then color the picture.

Trace each star.

Trace and write.

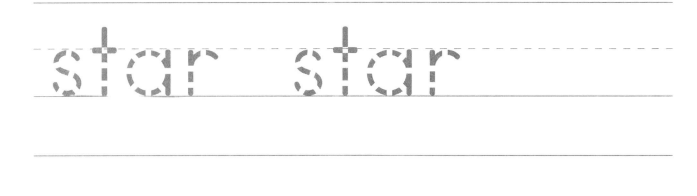

star star

Color each star yellow.

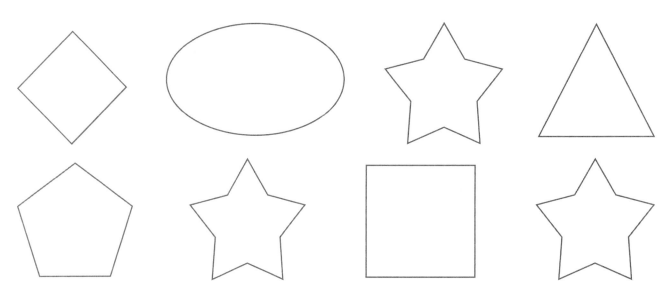

Trace the stars. Then color the picture.

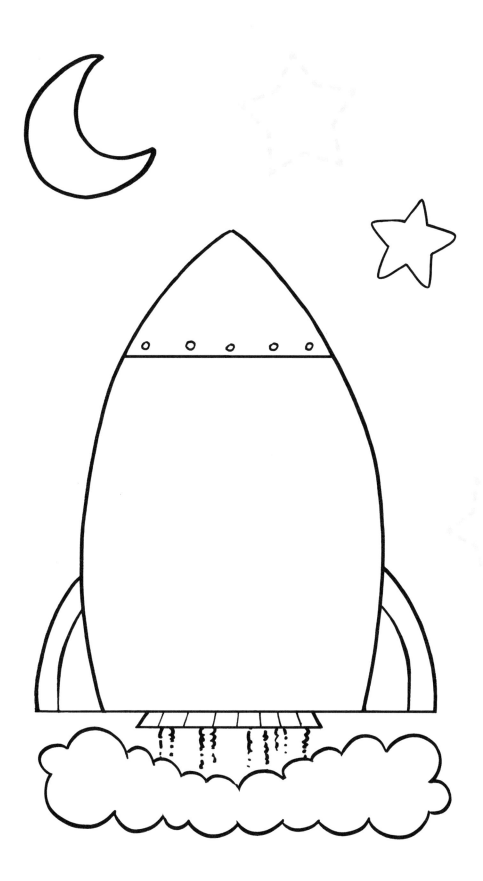

Trace each octagon.

Trace and write.

octagon

Color each octagon brown.

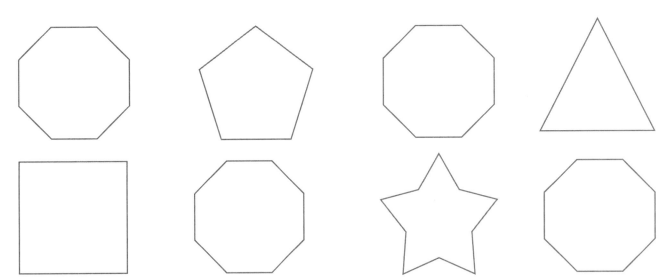

Trace the octagons. Then color the picture.

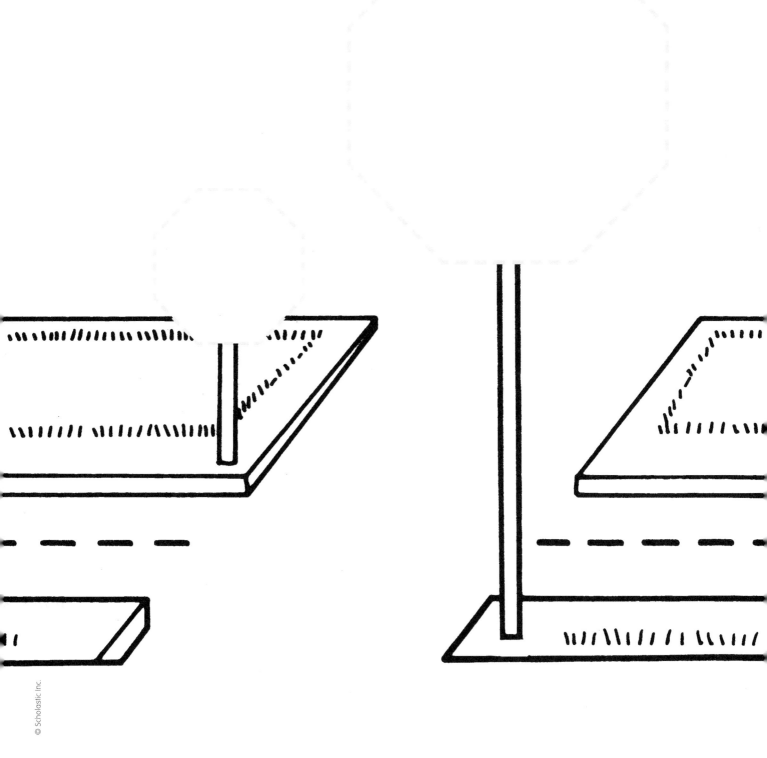

Color the picture. Use the color key.

blue   yellow   green   red

Draw a line to match the shape to its name.
Write the name.

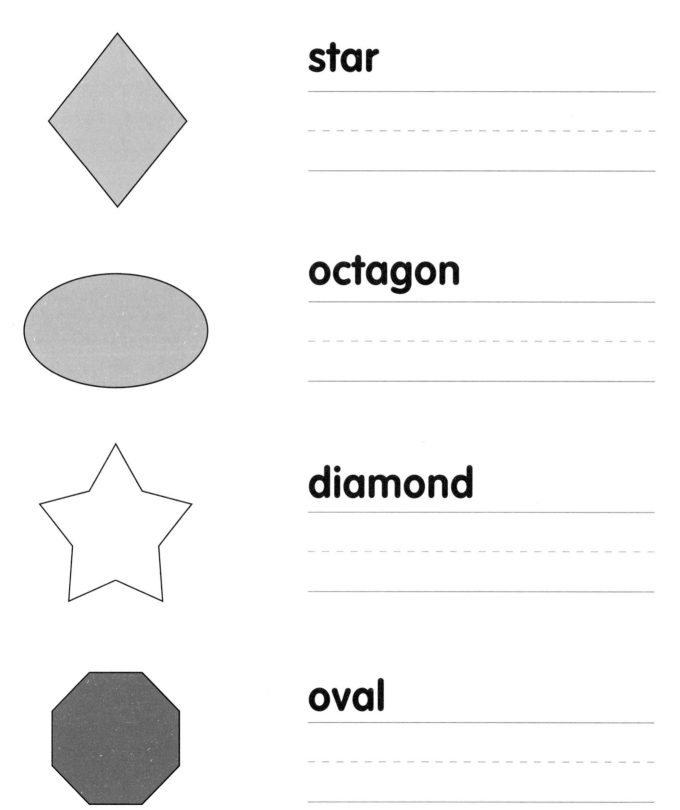

star

octagon

diamond

oval

Write the name for each shape.
Use the words in the box.

| square | diamond | octagon | triangle |

Write the name for each shape.
Use the words in the box.

circle   rectangle   oval   star

_____

- -

_____

_____

- -

_____

_____

- -

_____

_____

- -

_____

Color the picture. Use the color key.

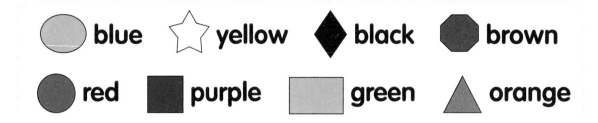